Legally Righteous

By

Dr. J.C. Wheeler

Pastor

New Life Worship Center

Warner Robins, GA

Jesus Is Lord

Unless otherwise indicated, all scripture quotations are taken from the **King James Version** of the Holy Bible.

Legally Righteous – Rediscovering the Righteousness of Christ
ISBN 1-59916-129-X
Copyright © 2006 Dr. J.C. Wheeler
PMB 301
1114 Hwy 96 C-1
Kathleen, GA 31047

Published by *New Life Worship Center of our Lord Jesus Christ, Inc.*
2301 Moody Road
Warner Robins, GA 31098

Senior Editor: Audrey Honan
Copy Editor: Kimberley Wheeler, Zazaca Menefee
Cover Design: Dr. J.C. Wheeler

For more information, contact:
    New Life Worship Center: (478) 922-7025
    Or visit: **www.pastorwheeler.com**

Printed in the United States of America. All rights reserved under international Copyright Law. Contents and/or cover may not be reproduced in whole or in part in any form without the express written consent of the Publisher.

TABLE OF CONTENTS

Forward 5

1 The Righteousness of God 7

2 Adam Reveals Righteousness 11

3 Abraham Reveals Righteousness 29

4 Moses reveals God's Righteous Law 37

5 The Righteousness of Christ 51

6 The Benefits of Righteousness..................71

7 Scripture Index 74

8   Righteous Confessions 90

9   Salvation Prayer and Confession................91

10 Illustration Charts 93
    Adam's Benefits from righteousness 94
    The Righteousness of God 95
    Three Things Adam Lost 96
    Adam's Two Positions 97
    Abraham's Chapters..........................98
    The Righteousness of Christ 99

Forward

Christ paid for our right to be legally righteous. He paid our sin debt, lived without sin, and resurrected from the dead. Through Christ, we have a contract agreement to participate in the power of God, because of the blood and the righteousness of Jesus Christ. The time has come for us to learn our rights and start walking in the righteousness of God. Many believers fail to receive the benefits of the righteousness of God, because of our sin consciousness. A sin consciousness resists the free flow of righteousness.

As Christians we have the potential of walking in the righteousness of God which will open up heaven for us. Once received, righteousness will guide us into the power of God. God wants to extend his power to righteous men in the earth. When God looks at the earth he is not looking for perfect Christians, but righteous Christians. If we are righteous then we are perfect candidates to use the power of God.

The righteousness of God is not an emotional thing, though it may cause an emotional reaction. With God, righteousness is a systematic process; it is written in heaven and it is very legal. There are some contracts God made which are so binding; God is watching the universe to ensure they have heavens endorsement. The righteousness of God is one such contract.

Since the foundation of the earth, man has never been capable of being righteous in the earth. From the beginning of time man has always failed at pleasing God and fulfilling his righteous cause. Through Jesus Christ, God finally got what he was looking for in the earth; a righteous man. Jesus was God, but he was also a righteous man. Since Jesus Christ was successful at living and walking in righteousness; God gave him full access to all his power.

We now have the awesome opportunity to walk through the righteous gateway Christ opened for us. We can give Jesus our sin, and receive his righteousness.

CHAPTER 1

THE RIGHTEOUSNESS OF GOD

Romans 3:21 says, ***But now the <u>righteousness of God</u> without the law is manifested, being witnessed by the law and the prophets; 22 Even the <u>righteousness of God</u> [which is] by faith of Jesus Christ unto all and upon all them that believe: for there is no difference:***

- Manifested – To make clear or visible
- Witnessed – To have seen or heard

- The law was a vehicle to carry the righteousness of God
- Faith seals God's righteousness in man

Over eight times the Bible gives attention to the phrase the "righteousness of God." The word righteousness can be defined as right ways or right doings. Though the phrase "righteousness of God" is only used a few times in the Bible; the reference is used over seven-hundred times in the Bible. It is safe to conclude, the idea of righteousness is a key theological principle to Christianity and the Holy Bible.

God has his own standard of what is right and his own way of doing things; it's called the "righteousness of God." Standing in opposition to God's way of doing things is the devils way and mans way of doing things. God finds it important through the scriptures to point out that his way of doing things is more profitable than man's ways.

In the Old Testament, God first began to reveal his righteousness through Adam. God gave Adam his way of doing things and as long as Adam did it God's way he prospered. When Adam started doing things his own way he failed to prosper.

God further revealed his righteousness through Abraham. We see through the scriptures how Abraham was able to gain God's righteousness through his faith because of his actions we now know him as the "father of faith." The Apostles will later use Abraham as a perfect example of how to receive the Righteousness of Christ by faith.

God then revealed his righteousness to the world through the Law of Moses. In the Law of Moses God expressed all of his desires for man. If man obeyed each law in the covenant, God would then bestow certain blessings upon him. The law helped man to see what God required, however man discovered it was very hard to keep every point without fail.

In the New Testament, God comes to the earth to demonstrate how to live God's way. Jesus Christ, God manifested, is the perfect expression of God's way of doing things. From his birth to his death, and through his resurrection, Jesus totally satisfied God's desire for a righteous man.

CHAPTER ONE

REVIEW

- God has his own standard of what is right and his own way of doing things; it's called the "righteousness of God."

- God gave Adam his way of doings things and as long as Adam did it God's way he prospered.

- We see through the scriptures how Abraham was able to gain God's righteousness through his faith because of his actions we now know him as the "father of faith."

- In the New Testament, God comes to the earth f to demonstrate how to live God's way.

CHAPTER 2

ADAM REVEALS RIGHTEOUSNESS

In the Old Testament, God first revealed his righteous way of doing things to the first man, Adam. God told Adam how to live and what to do in the garden. As long as Adam performed God's ways, he prospered. When Adam started doing things his own way, he failed.

Genesis 3:1 says, *"Now <u>the serpent was more subtil</u> than any beast of the field which the LORD God had made. And he said unto the woman, Yea, hath God said, Ye shall not eat of every tree of the garden?"*

- Subtil – to deal wisely

- The devil manifested himself through the serpent
- The enemy is sneaky and crafty
- Don't allow the devil to talk to you in your mind

Where did the devil (serpent) come from? God said he made everything and it was good. Something happened between Genesis 1:1, and 1:2. Jesus said he saw the devil fall like lightning. The devil tried to take over things in heaven so God cast him down to the earth.

Luke 10:18 says, *"And he said unto them, I beheld Satan as lightning fall from heaven."*

- Satan was created as servant to the LORD
- God cast him down to the earth after his rebellion
- Adam was given dominion over the devil in the earth

The devil was cast out of heaven to the earth, and when he hit the earth, his presence destroyed it.

God had to perform reconstructive surgery on the earth, to make it habitable by man. In Genesis we find three personalities in the earth; Adam, Eve, and the devil. Notice how God allowed the devil to reside in the earth, while giving man dominion over the earth.

From the beginning of creation, man was always supposed to rule the earth; but because of Adams failure, man lost his God given dominion. The last Adam, Jesus Christ, came on the scene as a man and took back the dominion of the earth.

God is trying to raise righteous dominion carriers, not babies. God wants righteous people who love him because they choose to love him. Righteous people who want to love him. Righteous people who love to love him. A righteous worshipper is what God is looking for.

John 4:23 says, ***"But the hour cometh, and now is, when the true worshippers shall worship the Father in spirit and in truth: for the Father seeketh such to worship him."***

- Spirit – the invisible part of man
- Truth – genuine

- God is looking for true worshippers

Let's get back to Genesis 3.

Genesis 3:1 says, *"Now <u>the serpent was more subtil</u> than any beast of the field which the LORD God had made. And he said unto the woman, Yea, hath God said, Ye shall not eat of every tree of the garden?"*

This verse says, the serpent (devil) was more "subtil" than any beast of the field. The word "subtil" means crafty. You can see how the enemy was very crafty in his dealings with Eve. First, he took on another form then what he really was. The devil is not a snake, but took on the form of a snake to deceive Eve. Second, he waited to talk to Eve while Adam was not around. The enemy knew he could not stand against them while they were unified. Finally, he tried to use God's command against Eve. He tried to make her think God was holding out on them and by following him they would become wise. He tries to keep us out of the righteousness of God, but Jesus Christ leads us into the righteous flow of God, through blood. The enemy can be very crafty, but as Christians we see right through his plans against us.

II Corinthians 2:11 says, *"Lest Satan should get an advantage of us: for we are not ignorant of his devices."*

- Advantage – to defraud or make gain of
- Ignorant – not knowing
- Devices – purposes and thoughts
- The enemy is constantly seeking opportunities to exploit us
- God gives us wisdom to see the enemy's strategies

Even the apostles of Christ had to seek God's direction in staying ahead of demonic strategies. For instance, Peter had to deal with the demonic activity in a man named Simon.

Acts 8:9 says, *"But there was a certain man, called Simon, which beforetime in the same city used sorcery, and bewitched the people of Samaria, giving out that himself was some great one:"*

- Sorcery - use of spells and occult powers
- Bewitched - to amaze and confuse
- Sorcery is a forbidden practice
- Notice the use of pride with sorcery

Without the cover of God's righteousness, we have no chance against the devil. But with the righteous blood covering in place, the devil cannot stop us. Even King David knew he was the best warrior around but he said to God I'm not going anywhere unless you go with me.

Genesis 3:1 says, *"...Now the serpent was more subtle than any beast of the field...."*

The serpent asked the woman if it was ok for her to eat from all the trees of the field. This was a tricky question because all he was trying to do was get her looking at the fruit of the tree.

The devil actually talked to the woman, and he will try and talk to you too. We cannot stop him from talking to us, but we can learn not to listen. If you listen to him long enough you may find yourself saying the same things he is saying. Job's wife fell into this same problem, by telling Job to curse God and die. She didn't make that up herself; she was quoting the same thing the devil said to God. We don't have time to confess the words of the devil.

Genesis 3:2-4 says, *"And the woman said unto the serpent, We may eat of the fruit of the trees of the garden: But of the fruit of the tree which [is] in the midst of the garden, God hath said, Ye shall not eat of it, neither shall ye touch it, lest ye die. And the serpent said unto the woman, Ye shall not surely die:"*

- Eve is talking with the enemy
- They all knew eating and touching the fruit was against God's commands
- Notice everyone's total disregard of God's commands to man

Notice how the devil is giving Eve words which are opposite of the Word of God. At this point, Eve should have just walked away, and totally discarded what the devil was saying, because it was not agreeing with the Word of God. The Word of God is always

17

true; reject any word which does not agree with the Word of God.

Genesis 3:5-9 says, *"For God doth know that in the day ye eat thereof, then your eyes shall be opened, and ye shall be as God's, knowing good and evil. And when the woman saw that the tree [was] good for food, and that it [was] pleasant to the eyes, and a tree to be desired to make [one] wise, she took of the fruit thereof, and did eat, and gave also unto her husband with her; and he did eat. And the eyes of them both were opened, and they knew that they [were] naked; and they sewed fig leaves together, and made themselves aprons. And they heard the voice of the LORD God walking in the garden in the cool of the day: and Adam and his wife hid themselves from the presence of the LORD God amongst the trees of the garden. And the LORD God called unto Adam, and said unto him, Where [art] thou?"*

- God only wanted man to know good
- Lust of the flesh, lust of the eyes, and the pride of life were the weapons used to attack Eve
- Sin causes us to hide from God

Adam was the general, the pastor, the president, and CEO of the earth. Whatever you choose to call him, he owned the earth. The enemy is subtle, and crafty, he realizes Adam controlled everything. He knew he could not attack him directly, because Adam was in a covenant relationship with God. Adam did not receive his instructions from God through a second or third party, but he got it directly from God.

The enemy was on a mission because he was cast out of heaven, and stripped of his former glory with God. He missed the previous glorious position he held with God. Since he found himself cast down to earth he set his sights on taking it over from Adam. The devil was there watching as God put Adam in charge, watching as God made Eve from Adam's rib. He was watching while God talked to the man and gave him dominion of the earth.

This explains how the devil knew what to ask the woman; he was watching the whole time. He heard everything that God told man and what the man told his wife. The devil saw that legally Adam owned, and controlled the earth, so he tried to find the easiest route do destroy the covenant shared between God and man.

He chose the woman as the target for his first attack, with the mindset to destroy their righteous standing with God. He wanted to get them to break covenant with God, and therefore break their righteous covering. Remember righteousness means being acceptable to God, and his soul aim was to make them unacceptable to God, to strip them of their power over the earth. He knew if they did not have power from God to control the earth, he could then step in and take over their dominion of the earth.

When Adam took of the fruit and ate; it was as if he got on his knees and said, enemy, now I worship you and I'll follow you. Adam's action can be compared to treason. Adam was not just a regular man sitting around at home; he was God's set man ruling the earth in God's instead. The one man ruling the earth chose to follow the devil. It was treason against God. If you commit treason you cannot just come back and say "Oh I'm sorry, I didn't mean it!"

In the military, if you commit treason, you cannot just come in and say, "I'm sorry, I didn't mean to give away those secrets." In the military you cannot just choose sides, and go back and forth based on whose fruit catches your eye that day. A person cannot shoot the gun from one side and then shoot from the other side the next day. No one on either side will trust you; they will both cast you out.

Adam's choice was a direct blow to mankind and the kingdom of God. He handed over everything God had given him to the devil's control. When he followed the devil, he submitted himself to the devil's plans, wishes, and desires. As a result the enemy gained control of everything he owned.

What did Adam own? He owned the whole world system. He owned the reproduction of man, he owned the animal kingdom, and controlled all farming operations.

The devil took control of all of these areas, and we can easily see the result of his hostile takeover today. All of this happened in a legal manner. It was not God's perfect will, but it was legal. We now see and experience rape, abuse, and neglect because of the earths new CEO; the devil. Man is in control but under the devil's authority. God in his sovereignty gave control to man, but man gave it over to the enemy. Since Adam gave it to the enemy it became a legal binding transfer.

Therefore, God will not go to the enemy and take the earth back because God is a contract God, since he gave the earth to Adam, Adam was free to do what he wanted with it. So God had to take his righteousness from Adam, and kick him out of Eden.

Three things Adam lost

- **Adam lost his righteousness**
- **Adam lost his earthly authority**
- **Adam lost his right to use heavenly authority**

Due to Adam's loss of righteousness the enemy was able to cripple Adam's sovereign reign over the earth. As stated earlier; when Adam obeyed the enemy he lost his right-standing with God. His disobedience stripped him of God's righteousness and of all his legal rights.

Genesis 3:7-8 says *"And the eyes of them both were opened, and they knew that they [were] naked; and they sewed fig leaves together, and made themselves aprons. And they heard the voice of the LORD God walking in the garden in the cool of the day: and Adam and his wife hid themselves from the presence of the LORD God amongst the trees of the garden."*

- Adam and Eve attempted to cover their own sin
- Adam chose leaves to cover his sin, but God would choose blood

In Genesis 3:7-8, we see evidence of their loss of righteousness. Several key words stand out: naked, leaves, and hid. After eating the fruit, they knew they were naked, so they sewed leaves together in order to cover themselves. After making aprons they hid from God behind the trees.

Genesis 3:21 says, **"Unto Adam also and to his wife did the LORD <u>God make coats of skins, and clothed them</u>."**

- An innocent animal lost its life to cover Adam's sin
- God performed the first animal sacrifice

Since they moved out from God's covering they immediately tried to cover themselves in their own way. The first thing he did was to use leaves to cover his sin, but God required innocent blood to cover sin. God killed any animal and clothed them with the skin of an innocent animal. This covering would allow man to still hear God, but he would no longer have fellowship with God like he once did. For this reason understanding our righteous position in Christ is so important.

The second thing Adam lost was his earthly authority. Prior to the fall, Adam controlled all operations in earth. He named the animals and kept the garden.

<u>*Earthly authority - Before the Fall*</u>

(His Righteous position)

Genesis 2:19 says, **"And out of the ground the LORD God formed every beast of the field, and every fowl of the air; and <u>brought [them] unto Adam</u> to see what <u>he would call them</u>: and whatsoever Adam every living creature, <u>that [was] the name</u> thereof."**

Genesis 2:15 says, *"And the LORD God took the man, and put him into the garden of Eden <u>to dress it and to keep it.</u>"*

- Adam named all the animals
- Adam dressed and kept the garden

<u>Earthly authority - After the Fall</u>

(His unrighteous position)

Genesis 3: 17-19 says *"And unto Adam he said, Because thou hast hearkened unto the voice of thy wife, and hast eaten of the tree, of which I commanded thee, saying, Thou shalt not eat of it: cursed [is] the ground for thy sake; in sorrow shalt thou eat [of] it all the days of thy life; Thorns also and thistles shall it bring forth to thee; and thou shalt eat the herb of the field; In the sweat of thy face shalt thou eat bread, till thou return unto the ground; for out of it wast thou taken: for dust thou [art], and unto dust shalt thou return."*

- God cursed the ground which was meant to bless him
- Thorns and thistles will make plant growth hard
- Adam has to sweat and work hard just to eat

The third thing Adam lost was his ability to exercise heavenly authority. Reducing him to work and live off the earthly system. Prior to his fall he worked in the heavenly system. In the heavenly system he had no earthly resistance. He also did not have to work for his food and living, it all came to him as a result of being righteous with God. When he needed a wife, God made him one, when he needed food, God's garden fed him; everything was provided for him; even a righteous vision of himself.

Adam gave up control of everything to the devil, but thank God for the last Adam, Jesus Christ who took back the power to rule the earth.

CHAPTER TWO

REVIEW

- As long as Adam performed God's ways, he prospered. When Adam started doing things his own way, he failed.

- From the beginning of creation, man was always supposed to rule the earth; but because of Adams failure, man lost his God given dominion.

- Without the cover of God's righteousness, we have no chance against the devil. But with the righteous blood covering in place the devil cannot stop us.

- Remember righteousness means being acceptable to God, and his soul aim was to make them unacceptable to God, to strip them of their power over the earth.

Dr. J.C. Wheeler

CHAPTER 3

ABRAHAM REVEALS RIGHTEOUSNESS

Romans 4:1-3 says, 1 What shall we say then that Abraham our father, as pertaining to the flesh, hath found?

2 For if Abraham were <u>justified</u> by works, he hath whereof to glory; but not before God.

3 For what saith the scripture? Abraham believed God, and it was <u>counted</u> unto him for righteousness.

- Counted – to reckon, to credit
- Justified – to pronounce righteous

- Works alone can never be enough to please God
- God gave Abraham righteousness because of his faith

God further reveals his righteousness through a man named Abraham. We can see through these verses how Abraham was able to gain God's righteousness through his faith. Abraham was not required to perform any work to get God's righteous, because any work he would have done would not have been enough to pay for righteousness. Abraham reveals to us that it is possible to become right with God without having to earn it. Abraham shows us that faith in God can bring any man into right standing with God, even if his works may not be perfect.

Romans 4:4-5 4 Now to him that worketh is the reward not <u>reckoned of grace</u>, but of <u>debt</u>.

5 But to him that worketh not, but believeth on him that justifieth the ungodly, his <u>faith</u> is counted for righteousness.

- Debt – that which is owed

- Grace – undeserved favor
- Reckoned – to count or credit
- Grace is a product of God's goodness
- Faith can be credited as righteousness

Abraham did not receive the righteousness of God because he worked for it. If there was any way he could work for it, then he would have the ability to earn enough righteousness to match all his labor. If he received righteousness as a product of his work then God has to pay him because God would be indebted to Abraham. God, being wiser than man, gave Abraham righteousness based on his measure of faith, instead of his works.

Romans 4:6-8 says, 6 Even as David also describeth the blessedness of the man, unto whom God <u>imputeth</u> righteousness without works,

7 Saying, Blessed are they whose iniquities are forgiven, and whose sins are covered.

8 Blessed is the man to whom the Lord will not impute sin.

- Impute – to credit to a persons account
- Imputed righteousness is given without good works
- Sin is imputed based on evil works

Man deserves death because of his sinful deeds, but to those who believe in God, they receive imputed righteousness. Imputed righteousness is just like receiving righteousness on credit. When you own a credit card, you can access money that does not belong to you nevertheless, it is credited to your account. Through Jesus Christ, we have been given righteousness we did not earn; it has been imputed to our heavenly account.

Romans 4:9-11 says, 9 Cometh this blessedness then upon the <u>circumcision</u> only, or upon the <u>uncircumcision</u> also? for we say that faith was reckoned to Abraham for righteousness.

10 How was it then reckoned? when he was in circumcision, or in uncircumcision? Not in circumcision, but in uncircumcision.

11 And he received the sign of circumcision, a seal of the righteousness of the faith which he had yet being uncircumcised: that he might be the father of all them that believe, though they be not circumcised; that righteousness might be imputed unto them also:

- Circumcision – those circumcised in the flesh
- Uncircumcision – those not circumcised in the flesh

Abraham helped the whole world come to the revelation of a marvelous truth; he found out that he could be made righteous by faith in God. To seal this covenant of faith, God gave Abraham the work of circumcision. Circumcision was the seal of the covenant that God made with Abraham, not the covenant itself. He received this sign while he was yet uncircumcised; therefore those who are of faith, not of the circumcision, can also walk in this truth of righteousness.

CHAPTER THREE

REVIEW

- Abraham was not required to perform any work to get God's righteous, because any work he would have done would not have been enough to pay for righteousness.

- Abraham shows us that faith in God can bring a man into right standing with God, even though his works may not be perfect.

- Man deserves death because of his sinful deeds, but to those who believe in God, they receive imputed righteousness.

- Through Jesus Christ we have been given righteousness we did not earn; it has been imputed to our heavenly account.

Dr. J.C. Wheeler

CHAPTER 4

MOSES REVEALS GOD'S RIGHTEOUS LAW

Exodus 24:12 says, *"And the **LORD said unto Moses**, Come up to me into the mount, and be there: and I will give thee tables of stone, and **a law, and commandments** which I have written; that thou mayest teach them."*

- Commandments - Moral and spiritual laws
- Mount - Mt. Sinai

God chose Moses to go and deliver the Israelites out of Egyptian bondage. Israel was in spiritual and natural bondage to the Egyptian way of living. They were not allowed to worship the God of their fathers, the God of Abraham, Isaac and Jacob, but forced to worship and give reverence to Egyptian God's and rituals.

God put in action a restoration plan to bring a fix to this bondage problem. God chose a man named Moses to go get the people out of Egypt and take them back to the land where Abraham once lived. Through great tribulation and mighty demonstrations of power Moses was successful at delivering the people from these two forms of bondage. Upon their release from Egypt he took them to Mt. Sinai.

At Mt. Sinai, God held several meetings with Moses, where he presented the sacred contract to the people of Israel. This contract required that they serve God and keep his commandments; and in return he would lift them up above all nations, guaranteeing them great success. Without reservation the people gladly accepted God's offer and received his commandments for living.

God supplied them with commandments to teach them how to live God's way. The Israelites had lived so long under Egyptian control that they only knew their way of living. Many of the Egyptian practices would have been in direct violation to God's standards of living. So God provided a simple list, Ten Commandments, which would help guide the people into God's righteousness. As long as they obeyed the commands they would be in good standing with God and would receive his righteous covering.

If they failed to obey the commands, God would be forced to remove his righteous covering.

Exodus 28:36 says, *"and thou shalt make a plate [of] pure gold, and grave upon it, [like] the engravings of a signet, <u>HOLINESS TO THE LORD</u>."*

- Holiness- separated to service for God
- God gave Moses instructions how to cover Israel's sin
- Aaron; Christ type as he wore his holy head covering
- Aaron would receive holiness for the whole congregation

Holiness is a product of righteousness, and is not just how we dress, where we go or our denomination affiliation. It is not in a specific suit style, hair style, or music style. If holiness was any of those things, then it would be man that produces holiness instead of God. Holiness is simply the fruit of a man or woman's righteous life.

True holiness manifests itself in a believer's life style, based on the righteousness of Christ. Holiness will affect how we act, where we go, and what we decide to put on. Holiness is a product of the righteousness of God that comes by faith when a person believes they are righteous. When we walk in the righteousness of Christ, holiness and sanctification manifest automatically.

Therefore, true acts of holiness will manifest themselves freely and not only because of dress standards in the local church. We will dress holy because we believe we are righteous. Those who are really sanctified, quickly agree with dress standards set in the local.

In Exodus 28, God told Aaron to gather the high priest garments that will be required to serve in his priestly office. He also told him to write some interesting words on it "Holiness to the Lord." Let's examine this inscription a little further by reading verse 38.

Exodus 28:38 says, ***"And it shall be upon Aaron's forehead, that Aaron may bear the iniquity of the holy things, which the children of Israel shall hallow in all their holy gifts; <u>and it shall be always upon his forehead, that they may be accepted before the LORD.</u>"***

- Hallow – to consecrate
- Aaron had to obey God's instructions to be accepted
- We cannot make up our own laws of righteousness
- We can only be righteous in Jesus Christ

The last part of verse 38 makes it clear that the words "Holiness to the LORD" was required to be worn on the High Priest's head covering to guarantee acceptance with the LORD. In other words, Aaron had to come before God with a head covering on that said, "Holiness to the LORD." When the hat was on he was considered Holy to the Lord, if he came in without the head covering, he would be considered unholy to the LORD.

This might seem strange in our eyes, but in the eyes of the Lord this made perfect sense and was serious business. The Priestly head covering, engraved with holiness to the Lord, represents the righteous covering we receive from Jesus Christ, by faith. Aaron did not have the blood of Jesus, so God used this inscription to foreshadow what Jesus would later perform for us. This idea was so important to God that if Aaron came in without the proper dress, God threatened to kill him.

I think it is important to note here, that true righteousness is not a product of our opinion. We do not have power to please God in the flesh, so we must appeal to his standards in order to be accepted. For Aaron, it meant wearing a big hat to church with "Holiness to the LORD" on it. For us today, it means believing in the Gospel of Christ, because when it comes to righteousness and holiness, we are in no position to negotiate the terms of his covenant.

It is amazing that Aarons big hat, on or off never really morally changed what Aaron really was. What was Aaron really? According to scripture, before he became High Priest, he was a cow worshipper.

Exodus 32:5 says, *"And when Aaron <u>saw [it]</u>, he built <u>an altar before it</u>; and Aaron made proclamation, and said, To morrow [is] a feast to the LORD."*

- Proclamation – to speak out or preach
- Aaron initially supported idol worship
- Aaron helped direct the idol worship services
- God still found a way to turn him around and use him as a Christ type

Aaron was a cow worshipper! When he had his priest head covering on, he was considered "holiness to the Lord," head covering off… instant cow worshipper! This statement may be a little extreme but, I think the idea of it gives us a picture of the reality of Aaron righteousness without God.

- Aaron was accepted with the LORD when he obeyed God's righteous plans for his generation

- Have you obeyed God's plans for you through Jesus Christ?

Exodus 28:38 says, ***"And it shall be upon Aaron's forehead, that Aaron may bear the iniquity of the holy things, which the children of Israel shall hallow in all their holy gifts; <u>and it shall be always upon his forehead, that they may be accepted before the LORD.</u>"***

Notice the use of the word "they" in the last part of this verse, the "they" represented Israel and Aaron. Aaron performed his High Priest duties to make himself and the whole nation of Israel righteous. Righteousness can also be defined as the state of being acceptable to God. Therefore the work of this one man Aaron made the whole nation righteous, every year, instantaneously.

Now based on Exodus 28, I want to establish two points. First, if Aaron obeyed God he would have a legal right to be accepted by God, based on God's words to him in Exodus 28. So when Aaron would enter in the tabernacle, God was obligated to accept him, and whatever God says, he must perform it because, it's impossible for him to lie.

Hebrews 6:18 says, *"That by two **immutable** things, in which [it was] **impossible for God to lie**, we might have a strong **consolation**, who have fled for refuge to lay hold upon the hope set before us:"*

- Immutable – not subject to or able to change
- Consolation – encouragement or comfort
- God can not ever lie
- If what he says does not exist, it will appear when he says it
- God's words hold creative power

Hebrews 6:18, validates the principle that everything God says is legally binding, therefore Aaron was able to step right into the Holy place where the cloud overshadowed the angels, and take a look. He has this legal right based on his purpose and God's words to him.

If we can see Aaron walking in this great benefit of God, how much more can we who have gained this legal right to participate in the blood covenant of Jesus Christ? If an angel would try to stop Aaron he could say, "Hey, move out of the way angel, I got business in the Holy place." The angel would not be able to say anything, or stop him because he is walking in his covenant promise. There is more written about us in the New Testament than there is written about Aaron, so if we understand this principle and how it works with Aaron, surely we can see the possibilities of it operating in us through the blood of Jesus.

My second point is, Israel also had a legal right to be accepted by God, but only through Aaron's work. If Aaron failed on his side of the covenant, Israel would not be considered acceptable before the Lord. This should remind us of Jesus Christ's work on the cross, he did all the work and, we have become righteous by his work.

Romans 5:17 says, ***"For if by one man's offence death reigned by one; much more they which receive abundance of grace and of the gift of righteousness shall <u>reign in life by one, Jesus Christ</u>."***

- Reign – the exercise of authority
- Adam's sin brought us (death) separation from God

- Jesus restored our relationship with God
- Righteousness causes us to reign in this life by Jesus

Hebrews 3:1 says, ***"Wherefore, holy brethren, <u>partakers</u> of the heavenly calling, consider the Apostle and <u>High Priest of our profession, Christ Jesus;</u>"***

- Partakers – to cooperate in activity
- Profession – to announce or confess
- Aaron is called to be the high priest
- Jesus Christ is called to be our high priest
- We are called to enjoy the fruit of Jesus' priesthood

Jesus is accepted by God because he is righteous, sinless, and holy, and because of this we are accepted by God through the righteousness of Christ.

Aaron is a type of Christ, and the more you see how Aaron brought Israel into God's righteousness, the more it will become clear how Jesus can bring us into this same righteousness. Aaron's position as High Priest for Israel is a perfect example of what Jesus has done for us. So remember, the righteousness of God through Christ is a legal, binding contract, based on the blood of Jesus Christ.

Legally Righteous

CHAPTER FOUR

REVIEW

- So God provide a simple list of Ten Commandments that would help guide the people into God's righteousness.

- Holiness is a product of righteousness, and is not just how we dress, where we go or our denomination affiliation.

- True holiness manifests itself in a believers life style based on the righteousness of Christ in their life.

- If Aaron failed on his side of the covenant, Israel would not be acceptable before the Lord. This should remind us of Jesus Christ's work on the cross; Jesus did all the work and, have become we were righteous by his work.

Dr. J.C. Wheeler

CHAPTER 5

THE RIGHTEOUSNESS OF CHRIST

God has not called me to preach about sin, why should I preach about something Jesus Christ already took care of on the cross? Jesus already destroyed the body of sin on the cross.

Romans 6:6 states, ***"Knowing this, that our old man is <u>crucified</u> with [him], that the <u>body of sin might be destroyed</u>, that henceforth we should not <u>serve</u> sin."***

- Crucified – to kill or renounce
- Serve – to be in bondage to
- Our old man was killed on the cross with Christ

- We no longer serve our old sin nature
- Sin is no longer our master

Romans 8:10 states, ***"And if Christ [be] in you, the body [is] dead because of sin; but the Spirit [is] life because of righteousness."***

- Sin caused us death and separation from God
- The Spirit brought us life
- Righteousness flows where the life of Jesus is

Based on these two verses, I would like to lift up the finished work of redemption that happened at the cross of, our Lord Jesus Christ. You can see the Apostle Paul using the knowledge of Christ's redemptive work, to launch us into another promise of God; the righteousness of God.

I Corinthians 5:21 states, ***"For he hath made him [to be] sin for us, who knew no sin; that we might be made the righteousness of God in him".***

- Jesus never sinned, he was perfect
- Jesus took our sin and became sin for us
- Jesus gave us his righteous, position with God

Paul's teaching shows us that Jesus took our sins to the cross, so that we may take Christ's righteousness to the world. We have been made the righteousness of God, because Jesus took away our sin.

John 10:10 states, ***"The thief cometh not, but for to steal, and to kill, and to destroy: I am come <u>that they might have life</u>, and that they might <u>have [it] more abundantly</u>"***

- Abundantly – ever increasing measures
- The enemy come to: steal, kill, and destroy your life
- Jesus came to give you the good life
- God wants you to live a successful life

The Greek word for life, in John 10:10 is Zoë. Zoë means the life of God. Therefore we can say that Jesus wants us to live the life of God and live it abundantly. The Vine's Expository Dictionary of New Testament Words defines Zoë this way: Zoë, "is used in the NT of life as a principle, life in the absolute sense, life as God has it, that which the Father has in Himself, and which He gave to the Incarnate Son to have in Himself, Jhn 5:26, and which the Son manifested in the world, 1Jo 1:2."

The righteousness of Christ is a legal binding contract which was sealed in the blood of Jesus Christ. Therefore we have the legal right to live the life (abundant life) of God, without the influence of the devil. It seems clear to me that God's intentions are that we live the good life. Let's break the redemptive work of Christ down to see the legal process of God's righteousness upon us.

Seven steps of redemption leading to righteousness

1. God became a man.
2. Christ manifested
3. Jesus was 100% God.
4. Jesus was 100% man.
5. Jesus went to the cross.
6. Jesus was resurrected
7. We are resurrected with him by faith.

Since we have given Jesus our sin; he has given us his righteousness. Therefore, we stand in God's righteousness, not because we've been good or will ever be good, but because we believed and received the Gospel of Christ, and the work of the cross. We see, our belief in Jesus Christ causes an automatic transfer of the righteousness of Christ to come on us by our faith. The righteousness of God through Jesus Christ is a legal, binding contract.

Many people believe sin will send people to hell, and that the power of sin is destroying the world. If this belief in sin is so strong in people, how much more should they trust in the righteousness of God? If you can believe that sin brings condemnation, guilt, and separation from God; then what do you suppose might happen to a person when the righteousness of God shows up their life?

There are those who believe all of these things about sin so much that they watch other people to see if they have sinned. Notice how the knowledge of sin has programmed us and if this knowledge of sin has produced certain strongholds in our mind, I wonder what the introduction of the knowledge of God's righteousness will do for us. Thank God for his mercy, because we have allowed ourselves to become so sin programmed. If sin can hold you pressed on the ground so much so that you can feel its pressure, how much more will the righteousness of God lift you up?

Thank God that this very important covenant was not left in your or my hands, instead God directly made it with Jesus Christ through the cross. God has made covenants with many people in the scriptures, but you and I don't carry our own personal covenant. Therefore, as Christians we cannot just make things up as we go along, we must seek instruction. If we desire success as Christians, we must learn how to legally tap into the Biblical covenants that allow us participative rights.

There are several covenants in the Bible that grant the believer participative rights, but for the purpose of receiving righteousness, the blood covenant of Jesus Christ is only one for us.

In I Corinthians 11:25, Paul said, "*After the same manner also [he took] the cup, when he had supped, saying, This cup is <u>the new testament in my blood</u>: this do ye, as oft as ye drink [it], in remembrance of me.*"

- Testament – contract, or agreement
- Jesus drank the cup of wrath that was meant for us

- The cross marked the beginning of a new contract from God
- Communion brings this blood contract back to remembrance

The *Vine's Expository Dictionary of New Testament Words*, defines the word "testament" or covenant as a word which "...signifies a mutual undertaking between two parties or more, each binding himself to fulfill obligations, it does not in itself contain the idea of joint obligation, it mostly signifies an obligation undertaken by a single person."

Adam was given a contract because God needed him to be a Christ type in order to exercise physical dominion over the earth. Noah was given a contract because God needed him to be a Christ type to save the destiny of the world. Abraham was given a contract because God needed him to be a Christ type who would start a new nation of believers. The Israelites fell under Abraham's contract because they were his direct descendents.

The gentile people had no promise, no covenant, and no blessing. We don't have a personal contract with God. So, if you are going get anything from God, you got to get it through someone else's contract. None of us have ever been elevated to a right position with God, in the sense that we can sit with God and negotiate a fellowship contract. However through Jesus Christ we can participate in his blood covenant made with God, because it was made to give us a part in the blessing.

We receive this promise of righteousness through the blood covenant of Christ. We are the righteousness of God through Christ, and our righteousness has been sealed through our faith. It will forever be enforced, when we choose to believe that we are righteous through Jesus.

Romans 3:22 says, ***"Even the <u>righteousness</u> of God [which is] by faith of Jesus Christ unto all and <u>upon all them that believe:</u> for there is no difference:"***

- God has his own ideas about how man should live

- God's ways of living is called God's righteousness
- Jesus fulfilled God's way of living right for us

Rom 10:10 says, *"For with the heart man <u>believeth unto righteousness</u>; and with the mouth <u>confession</u> is made unto salvation."*

- Confession – to speak openly
- We no longer have to work to be righteous
- Jesus worked to be righteous for us
- We believe our way into righteousness

Righteousness is enforced even when you don't feel like it! It is enforced whether you have been good or bad. It is enforced whether things are going right or wrong for you, it is enforced! The power and force of righteousness, is in the purity of the blood of Jesus, and your belief in the work of redemption by Christ.

I Corinthians 1:30 says, **But of him are ye in Christ Jesus, who of God is made unto us wisdom,** *and righteousness, and sanctification, and redemption:*

- Jesus Christ became righteousness for us
- We walk in righteousness through his right-standing with God

II Corinthians 5:21 says, *"For he hath made him [to be] sin for us, who knew no sin; that we might be made the righteousness of God in him."*

- Christ took on our sin
- We take on Christ righteousness

Since the righteousness of God is upon us; the devil cannot control us like he once did. There are four things the devil can no longer do to us unless we allow him.

- <u>Number 1</u>: The devil cannot influence our lives unless we allow him; we are not part of his world system.
- <u>Number 2</u>: The devil cannot steal our blessings unless we allow him.

- <u>Number 3</u>: The devil cannot stop our ministry unless we allow him.
- <u>Number 4</u>: The devil cannot stop our prosperity from overtaking us unless we allow him.

Here is a wonderful confession for us to make, "My state of being acceptable to God, just like Jesus, is a legal binding contract between God and Jesus Christ based on his blood." If we do not make conclusions like this, we will find it hard to live in the righteousness of God. It is just my conclusion, based on what he is teaching me, and since I'm teaching you, I thought I would put it out there for you to confess it yourself.

Righteousness can also be defined as the state of being acceptable to God or God's right-ways-of-living. Since it is impossible for us to produce righteousness by our own works, we must therefore get it from someone who can. Our only option or source of true righteousness is Jesus Christ. Since we are covered in God's righteous; when he looks at us, he no longer sees us, but the blood of Jesus Christ his righteous son.

I Corinthians 11:25 again says, ***"After the same manner also [he took] the cup, when he had supped, saying, This cup is the <u>new testament in my blood</u>: this do ye, as oft as ye drink [it], in remembrance of me."***

- God made a new contract or testament with Jesus
- Jesus fulfilled his part by completing the cross work
- God fulfilled his part by granting salvation
- We fulfill our part when we believe in Jesus Christ

Notice Paul's use of the word "new," he says it is a, "new testament." We are all familiar with the use of these two words in relationship to the structure and cannon of our Holy Bible. We have learned that there is a New Testament section and an Old Testament section in the Bible.

However, in I Corinthians 11:25, were not talking about a section of the Bible. This verse is identifying a "new testament" based on the blood of Jesus, which was set up by God himself. As we stated earlier, a testament is a covenant or contract. So the Bible is teaching us that we have a new covenant, a new contract, or a new agreement with God, based on Christ's blood.

The old contract was based on man's ability, or lack thereof, to be morally righteous before God. The old one was based on the law of God, and the flesh of man. The law represented God position, and the flesh represented man position. Man would have to make his flesh obey the law of God, and in return would reap forgiveness, righteousness and fellowship with God. The benefits of the law were extracted based on fleshly obedience to the law of God. The new contract would be based on Jesus Christ ability to be righteous before God, allowing us participative rights.

God and Jesus Christ are the two contracting parties; and as we stand, watch, and believe, we reap all the great benefits. God wrote us out of the operational side of the contract, so we have nothing to do with its fulfillment.

If God had not written us out, our righteousness, salvation, and prosperity would depend solely on our lust, our depression, our madness, and our craziness. Thank God he wrote us out and gave us the right to participate only. He wrote us out but then he picked us back up later.

So stop basing your fate on your feelings. God brings success to the righteous, and according to the blood of Jesus we are righteous. Faith will work whether we feel it or not. Our feelings have never produced anything for us except worry.

I Corinthians 11:25 says, we have a new testament; a new contract, a new covenant, and new arrangement, in the blood of Jesus. So we can conclude, that the righteousness of God acts as a contractual arrangement between God and Jesus

Christ, therefore, making us the righteousness of God, in Christ Jesus. Now that we have learned we are the righteousness of God, let's start speaking about ourselves the way the Bible does. Remember, we are righteous by the blood of Jesus Christ, not by good works.

The only way God could get the earth back was to come as a man. A regular man would not do; God would have to become a man so he could equally represent God, and man. Jesus, who is God, came as a man born under the Mosaic Covenant. He received a prophetic anointing to preach the Kingdom of God, while under the Old Covenant, but he was almighty God. He ministered as a prophet under the old covenant but he was God in the flesh. Notice how God produced a legal way to enter the earth, by becoming a man. He lived 100% without sin which meant now there was a legally righteous man in the earth. Eternal righteousness returned to earth through our Savior Jesus Christ.

God's desire for a righteous man was finally satisfied; because Jesus was the first man to ever satisfy the righteous requirements of the law. Jesus went to the cross and died, taking on the sin of man. Three days later he resurrected, so we could be justified through his work on the cross. Jesus brought back God's righteousness to the earth, and that's why the Bible calls him the last Adam.

Revelation 1:18 says, *"I [am] he that liveth, and was dead; and, behold, I am alive for evermore, Amen; and <u>have the of hell and of death.</u>"*

- This is a vision of the resurrected Christ
- Jesus has all power in heaven and in Earth

During the three days Jesus was in the grave he went down and grabbed the keys to hell and death. What Jesus did was all legal; Adam lost control of the earth, but Jesus came back legally as the last Adam and took control of everything when he resurrected, taking us to glory with him.

Hebrews 2:10 says, *"For it became him, for whom [are] all things, and by whom [are] all things, in bringing <u>many sons unto glory</u>, to make the captain of their salvation perfect through sufferings."*

- Captain – highest officer in chief command
- Perfect – completion of an accomplishment
- All things were made by Jesus

- All things were made for Jesus
- Jesus brought the sons of God to heavenly places when he resurrected

Ephesians 2:5-6 says, *"Even when we were dead in sins, hath <u>quickened us</u> together with Christ, (by grace ye are saved;) And hath <u>raised [us]</u> up together, and <u>made [us] sit</u> together in heavenly [places] in Christ Jesus:"*

- Quickened – to make live
- Our sins made us dead (separated from) God
- Christ made us alive together
- Christ raised us together
- Christ made us sit together

Again what Jesus did was legal; because he sealed our redemption with his blood, through which we have a legal binding contract that says we can be made righteous. This new contract sealed through Jesus' blood defines all our rights as believers, but for this chapter we are only focusing on righteousness. Now that we have learned we are righteous in the blood of Jesus Christ; there are wonderful benefits we have right's to, and all these rights are legally ours because of Christ.

Hebrews 2:14 says, *"Forasmuch then as the children are partakers of flesh and blood, he also himself likewise took part of the same; that through death he might destroy him that had the power of death, that is, the devil;"*

- In Jesus Christ, God experienced being a man
- The Devil's power over the believer is destroyed

The last Adam, Jesus Christ, came and took back the power of death; he did this legally as a man. The righteous of God through Christ is a legal binding contract. Adam legally lost righteousness, but Christ the last Adam legally brought righteousness back.

Jesus conquered the greatest enemy to man; death. Death has been sowing fear in the world since the beginning of Adam's fall. Fear fights against the faith of God in mankind. Without faith no man can please God, so man was continually outside of God because of fear. Jesus destroyed the fear of death by conquering fear through the resurrection from death.

Philippians 2:10 says, **That at the name of Jesus every knee should bow, of [things] in heaven, and [things] in earth, and [things] under the earth;**

- Jesus is the name above every name
- All three worlds bow at his name
- Everyone will eventually bow, freely or by force

As you know, the devil is still here operating in the world and through the system of this world, but has nothing to do with you and the Kingdom of God. Because Jesus resurrected and conquered death, the devil no longer has control of death. This is why Jesus said, those who believe in me would never die. Of course our bodies will be translated into a new body, but we will not participate with the spirit of death. Paul said, to be absent from the body, is to be present with the Lord.

The last Adam came to take over all the power of the devil, and received all power in heaven and earth. How was Jesus able to take all the power? Jesus was 100% man, and 100% God and he fulfilled the righteous requirements of law and God. There was no law the devil could accuse Jesus of, therefore the devil could not legally defeat him because he was a legal, perfect, righteous descendant of Adam.

We are not in the devil's kingdom or world. Therefore we are not under the devil's control or influence. We are not under his principles, plans or system. We are one with Jesus Christ, the Lord, and under his control, his principles and his system. We are translated out of the kingdom of darkness into the Kingdom of Light or the Kingdom of his dear son.

CHAPTER FIVE
REVIEW

- We have been made the righteousness of God because Jesus took away your sin.

- The righteousness of Christ is a legal binding contract which was sealed in the blood of Jesus Christ.

- True holiness manifests itself in a believers life style based on the righteousness of Christ in their life.

- If Aaron failed on his side of the covenant, Israel would not be acceptable before the Lord. This should remind us of Jesus Christ's work on the cross; Jesus did all the work and, have become we were righteous by his work.

CHAPTER 6

BENEFITS OF RIGHTEOUSNESS

Matthew 3:15 says, *"And Jesus answering said unto him, Suffer [it to be so] now: for thus it becometh us to <u>fulfil all righteousness</u>. Then he suffered him."*

Mark 1:10 says, *"And straightway coming up out of the water, he saw <u>the heavens opened</u>, and the Spirit like a dove descending upon him:"*

Righteousness gives us access to things in heaven. Only righteous men have access to things in heaven. The Bible records that when Jesus was baptized, the heavens opened to him. When the heavens opened, the Father gave witness that Jesus was his son. Jesus told John, he had to be baptized by him because it was necessary to fulfill all righteousness. When Jesus came out of the water, immediately the heavens opened up to Jesus. I believe righteousness is what gets heaven's attention.

II Chronicles 16:9 says, *"For the eyes of the LORD run to and fro throughout the whole earth, <u>to shew himself strong</u> in the behalf of [them] whose heart [is] perfect toward him."*

Righteousness also gives us kingdom support on the earth. God is looking for men on the earth with whom he can share his power. Righteousness qualifies us for use in the Father's earth dominion plans. When a natural boss is looking for someone to promote and give more authority, he will choose someone who is in good standing with himself and the company. I believe God will back men who are in good standing with him.

Additionally, Righteousness gives us the power to use the name of Jesus Christ. Anyone can pronounce the name of Jesus with their mouth, but only righteous men understand how to use the power of the name.

When a righteous man prays, the name of Jesus in him is activated by his faith. When God receives this kind of prayer it is as if Jesus Christ himself is praying, because the prayer is covered in the righteousness of Jesus. Righteousness brings the power of the name of Jesus to the believer's life.

We have examined how as Christians we are legally righteous. Legally! When you are righteous, it is your legal right to operate in the Kingdom of God. Righteousness opens up everything in the kingdom. The righteous of God, through Christ, is a legal, binding contract. We can now see ourselves as legally righteous; not based on our goodness, but on your belief in the finished work of the cross of Christ.

Dr. J.C. Wheeler

CHAPTER ONE
SCRIPTURE INDEX

Romans 3:21 says, *But now the <u>righteousness of God</u> without the law is manifested, being witnessed by the law and the prophets; 22 Even the <u>righteousness of God</u> [which is] by faith of Jesus Christ unto all and upon all them that believe: for there is no difference:*

CHAPTER TWO
SCRIPTURE INDEX

Genesis 3:1 says, *"Now <u>the serpent was more subtil</u> than any beast of the field which the LORD God had made. And he said unto the woman, Yea, hath God said, Ye shall not eat of every tree of the garden?"*

Luke 10:18 says, *"And he said unto them, I beheld Satan as lightning fall from heaven."*

John 4:23 says, *"But the hour cometh, and now is, when the true worshippers shall worship the Father in spirit and in truth: for the Father seeketh such to worship him."*

Genesis 3:1 says, *"Now <u>the serpent was more subtil</u> than any beast of the field which the LORD God had made. And he said unto the woman, Yea, hath God said, Ye shall not eat of every tree of the garden?"*

II Corinthians 2:11 says, *"Lest Satan should get an advantage of us: for we are not ignorant of his devices."*

Acts 8:9 says, *"But there was a certain man, called Simon, which beforetime in the same city used sorcery, and bewitched the people of Samaria, giving out that himself was some great one:"*

Genesis 3:1 says, *"...Now the serpent was more subtle than any beast of the field...."*

Genesis 3:2-4 says, *"And the woman said unto the serpent, We may eat of the fruit of the trees of the garden: But of the fruit of the tree which [is] in the midst of the garden, God hath said, Ye shall not eat of it, neither shall ye touch it, lest ye die. And the serpent said unto the woman, Ye shall not surely die:"*

Genesis 3:5-9 says, *"For God doth know that in the day ye eat thereof, then your eyes shall be opened, and ye shall be as God's, knowing good and evil. And when the woman saw that the tree [was] good for food, and that it [was] pleasant to the eyes, and a tree to be desired to make [one] wise, she took of the fruit thereof, and did eat, and gave also unto her husband with her; and he did eat. And the eyes of them both were opened, and they knew that they [were] naked; and they sewed fig leaves together, and made themselves aprons. And they heard the voice of the LORD God walking in the garden in the cool of the day: and Adam and his wife hid themselves from the* presence of the LORD God amongst the trees of the garden. And the LORD God called unto Adam, and said unto him, Where [art] thou?"

Genesis 3:7-8 says *"And the eyes of them both were opened, and they knew that <u>they [were] naked</u>; and they <u>sewed fig leaves together</u>, and made themselves aprons. And they heard the voice of the LORD God walking in the garden in the cool of the day: and Adam and his wife <u>hid themselves from the presence of the LORD</u> God amongst the trees of the garden."*

Genesis 3:21 says, *"Unto Adam also and to his wife did the LORD <u>God make coats of skins, and clothed them</u>."*

Genesis 2:19 says, *"And out of the ground the LORD God formed every beast of the field, and every fowl of the air; and <u>brought [them] unto Adam</u> to see what <u>he would call them</u>: and whatsoever Adam every living creature, <u>that [was] the name</u> thereof."*

Genesis 2:15 says, *"And the LORD God took the man, and put him into the garden of Eden <u>to dress it and to keep it</u>."*

Genesis 3: 17-19 says *"And unto Adam he said, Because thou hast hearkened unto the voice of thy wife, and hast eaten of the tree, of which I commanded thee, saying, Thou shalt not eat of it: cursed [is] the ground for thy sake; in sorrow shalt thou eat [of] it all the days of thy life; Thorns also and thistles shall it bring forth to thee; and thou shalt eat the herb of the field; In the sweat of thy face shalt thou eat bread, till thou return unto the ground; for out of it wast thou taken: for dust thou [art], and unto dust shalt thou return."*

CHAPTER THREE
SCRIPTURE INDEX

Romans 4:1-3 *says, 1 What shall we say then that Abraham our father, as pertaining to the flesh, hath found?*

2 For if Abraham were justified by works, he hath whereof to glory; but not before God.

3 For what saith the scripture? Abraham believed God, and it was counted unto him for righteousness.

Romans 4:4-5 *4 Now to him that worketh is the reward not reckoned of grace, but of debt.*

5 But to him that worketh not, but believeth on him that justifieth the ungodly, his faith is counted for righteousness.

Romans 4:6-8 *says, 6 Even as David also describeth the blessedness of the man, unto whom God imputeth righteousness without works,*

7 Saying, Blessed are they whose iniquities are forgiven, and whose sins are covered.

8 Blessed is the man to whom the Lord will not impute sin.

Romans 4:9-11 *says, 9 Cometh this blessedness then upon the circumcision only, or upon the uncircumcision also? for we say that faith was reckoned to Abraham for righteousness.*

10 How was it then reckoned? when he was in circumcision, or in uncircumcision? Not in circumcision, but in uncircumcision.

11 And he received the sign of circumcision, a seal of the righteousness of the faith which he had yet being uncircumcised: that he might be the father of all them that believe, though they be not circumcised; that righteousness might be imputed unto them also:

CHAPTER FOUR
SCRIPTURE INDEX

Exodus 24:12 says, *"And the <u>LORD said unto Moses</u>, Come up to me into the mount, and be there: and I will give thee tables of stone, and <u>a law, and commandments</u> which I have written; that thou mayest teach them."*

Exodus 28:36 says, *"and thou shalt make a plate [of] pure gold, and grave upon it, [like] the engravings of a signet, <u>HOLINESS TO THE LORD.</u>"*

Exodus 28:38 says, *"And it shall be upon Aaron's forehead, that Aaron may bear the iniquity of the holy things, which the children of Israel shall hallow in all their holy gifts; <u>and it shall be always upon his forehead, that they may be accepted before the LORD.</u>"*

Exodus 32:5 says, *"And when Aaron <u>saw [it]</u>, he built <u>an altar before it</u>; and Aaron made proclamation, and said, To morrow [is] a feast to the LORD."*

Hebrews 6:18 says, *"That by two immutable things, in which [it was] <u>impossible for God to lie</u>, we might have a strong consolation, who have fled for refuge to lay hold upon the hope set before us:"*

Romans 5:17 says, *"For if by one man's offence death reigned by one; much more they which receive abundance of grace and of the gift of righteousness shall reign in life <u>by one, Jesus Christ</u>."*

Hebrews 3:1 says, *"Wherefore, holy brethren, partakers of the heavenly calling, consider the Apostle and <u>High Priest of our profession, Christ Jesus;</u>"*

Legally Righteous
CHAPTER FIVE
SCRIPTURE INDEX

Romans 6:6 states, *"Knowing this, that our old man is crucified with [him], that the <u>body of sin might be destroyed</u>, that henceforth we should not serve sin."*

Romans 8:10 states, *"And if Christ [be] in you, <u>the body [is] dead because of sin</u>; but the Spirit [is] life because of righteousness."*

I Corinthians 5:21 states, *"For he hath made <u>him [to be] sin for us</u>, who knew no sin; that we might be <u>made the righteousness of God in him"</u>.*

John 10:10 states, *"The thief cometh not, but for to steal, and to kill, and to destroy: I am come <u>that they might have life</u>, and that they might <u>have [it] more abundantly"</u>*

In I Corinthians 11:25, Paul said, " *After the same manner also [he took] the cup, when he had supped, saying, This cup is <u>the new testament in my blood</u>: this do ye, as oft as ye drink [it], in remembrance of me.*"

Romans 3:22 says, *"Even the righteousness of God [which is] by faith of Jesus Christ unto all and <u>upon all them that believe</u>: for there is no difference:"*

Rom 10:10 says, *"For with the heart man <u>believeth unto righteousness</u>; and with the mouth confession is made unto salvation."*

I Corinthians 1:30 says, *But of him are ye in Christ Jesus, who of God is made unto us wisdom, and righteousness, and sanctification, and redemption:*

II Corinthians 5:21 says, *"For he hath made him [to be] sin for us, who knew no sin; that we might be made the righteousness of God in him."*

I Corinthians 11:25 again says, *"After the same manner also [he took] the cup, when he had supped, saying, This cup is the <u>new testament in my blood</u>: this do ye, as oft as ye drink [it], in remembrance of me."*

Revelation 1:18 says, *"I [am] he that liveth, and was dead; and, behold, I am alive for evermore, Amen; and <u>have the of hell and of death</u>."*

Hebrews 2:10 says, *"For it became him, for whom [are] all things, and by whom [are] all things, in bringing <u>many sons unto glory</u>, to make the captain of their salvation perfect through sufferings."*

Ephesians 2:5-6 says, *"Even when we were dead in sins, hath <u>quickened us</u> together with Christ, (by grace ye are saved;) And hath <u>raised [us]</u> up together, and <u>made [us] sit</u> together in heavenly [places] in Christ Jesus:"*

Hebrews 2:14 says, *"Forasmuch then as the children are partakers of flesh and blood, he also himself likewise took part of the same; that through death he might destroy him that had the power of death, that is, the devil;"*

Philippians 2:10 says, That at the name of Jesus every knee should bow, of [things] in heaven, and [things] in earth, and [things] under the earth;

CHAPTER SIX
SCRIPTURE INDEX

Matthew 3:15 says, *"And Jesus answering said unto him, Suffer [it to be so] now: for thus it becometh us to <u>fulfil all righteousness</u>. Then he suffered him."*

Mark 1:10 says, *"And straightway coming up out of the water, he saw <u>the heavens opened</u>, and the Spirit like a dove descending upon him:"*

II Chronicles 16:9 says, *"For the eyes of the LORD run to and fro throughout the whole earth, <u>to shew himself strong</u> in the behalf of [them] whose heart [is] perfect toward him."*

Dr. J.C. Wheeler
RIGHTEOUSNESS
CONFESSIONS

I have a right to live a abundant, joyous, righteous life, without the devils influence.

I am saved by the pure, righteous, holy blood of Jesus Christ.

I am righteous through the blood of Jesus Christ, by my faith.

The righteousness of God is in me and upon me, because I am a son of God.

Everything I do, say, and touch will prosper because the righteousness of Christ is upon me.

Legally Righteous
SALVATION PRAYER AND CONFESSIONS

Salvation Prayer

Father, I come to you in the name of Jesus Christ. I am a sinner, in need of salvation and I am sorry for my sins. I need your forgiveness.

I believe that Jesus Christ shed his blood on the cross and died for my sins, and I turn from sin.

Right now I confess Jesus as the Lord of my life. I believe that God raised Jesus from the dead. I accept Jesus Christ as my Savior and I believe I am saved by the blood of Jesus.

Thank you Jesus for your grace which has saved me from my sins.

In Jesus name,

Dr. J.C. Wheeler
Salvation Confessions

Romans 10:9-10

9 That if thou shalt <u>confess with thy mouth</u> the Lord Jesus, and shalt believe in thine heart that God hath raised him from the dead, thou shalt be saved.

10 For with the heart man believeth unto righteousness; and <u>with the mouth confession</u> is made unto salvation.

Jesus Christ is my Lord and Savior.

I am born again by the blood of Jesus Christ, my deliverer and Savior.

I will live forever with Jesus Christ, because he saved me from hell and destruction.

Legally Righteous
ILLUSTRATION CHARTS

Adam Benefits from Righteousness

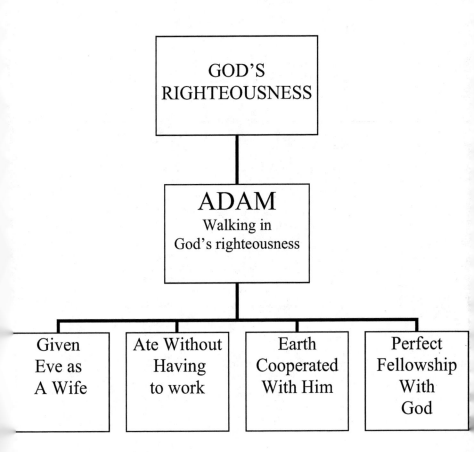

Dr. J.C. Wheeler
The Righteousness of God

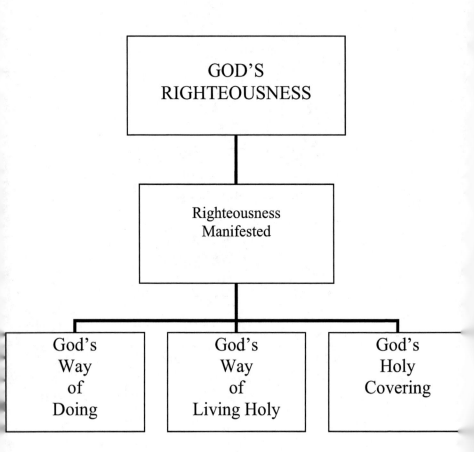

THREE THINGS ADAM LOST

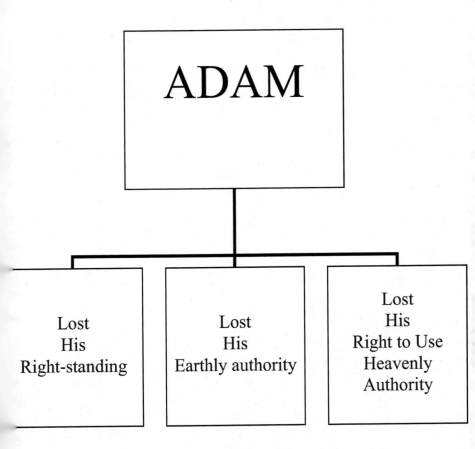

ADAM'S TWO POSITIONS

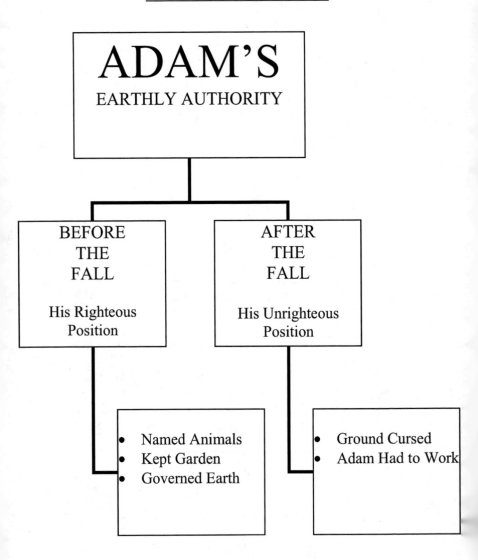

Legally Righteous
ABRAHAM'S CHAPTERS

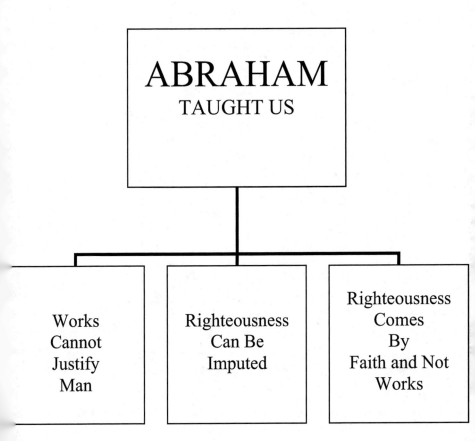

Dr. J.C. Wheeler

THE RIGHTEOUSNESS OF CHRIST

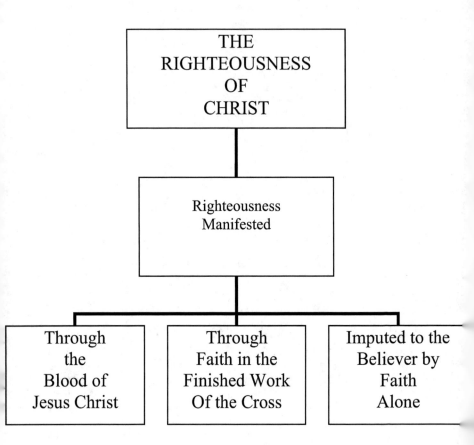

THE BENEFITS OF RIGHTEOUSNESS

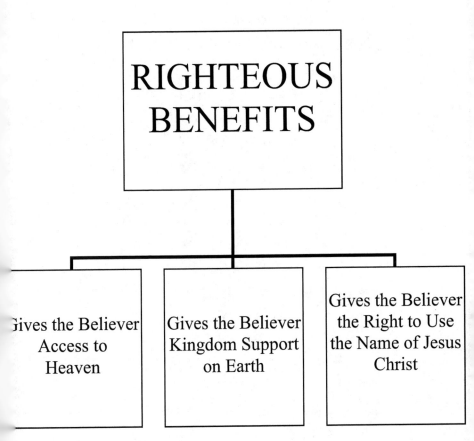

Dr. J.C. Wheeler

MINISTRY CONTACT

NEW LIFE WORSHIP CENTER

OF OUR LORD JESUS CHRIST INC.

2301 MOODY ROAD

WARNER ROBINS, GEORGIA

(478) 922-7025

WWW.NLWC-GA.COM

DR. J.C. WHEELER

AND

MINISTER KIMBERLEY WHEELER

PMB 301

1114 HWY 96 C-1

KATHLEEN, GA 31047

(478) 922-7025

WWW.PASTORWHEELER.COM

PASTORWHEELER@COX.NET